Studying Weather and Climates

by Conrad J. Storad

Science Content Editor:
Kristi Lew

Science content editor: Kristi Lew
A former high school teacher with a background in biochemistry and more than 10 years of experience in cytogenetic laboratories, Kristi Lew specializes in taking complex scientific information and making it fun and interesting for scientists and non-scientists alike. She is the author of more than 20 science books for children and teachers.

www.rourkepublishing.com

To Meghan. Never stop teaching!
-- CJS

Photo credits: Cover © leonid_tit, Plechi, firtad, Cover logo frog © Eric Pohl, test tube © Sergey Lazarev; Table of Contents © vichie81; Page 5 © Regien Paassen; Page 6 © rickt; Page 7 © Malte Pott; Page 9 © Jan Martin Will; Page 10 © Kevin Carden, Ari V; Page 11 © Armin Rose, Stephen Coburn; Page 12 © Eder, huyangshu; Page 13 © Daniel Loretto, Pi-Lens; Page 15 © Anton Prado PHOTO; Page 17 © Tony Campbell; Page 18 © lafoto; Page 19 © Dean Kerr; Page 20 © United States Air Force/Bo Joyner; Page 21 © Carolina K. Smith, M.D.

Editor: Kelli Hicks

Cover and page design by Nicola Stratford, bdpublishing.com

Library of Congress Cataloging-in-Publication Data

Storad, Conrad J.
 Studying weather and climates / Conrad J. Storad.
    p. cm. -- (My science library)
Includes bibliographical references and index.
ISBN 978-1-61741-749-8 (Hard cover) (alk. paper)
ISBN 978-1-61741-951-5 (Soft cover)
1. Climatology. 2. Weather. I. Title.
QC854.S76 2012
551.6--dc22
                        2011004762

Rourke Publishing
Printed in the United States of America,
North Mankato, Minnesota
060711
060711CL

www.rourkepublishing.com - rourke@rourkepublishing.com
Post Office Box 643328 Vero Beach, Florida 32964

Table of Contents

Weather or Climate?

Weather and **climate** shape the world in which we live.

Weather is the current condition of the atmosphere. It includes temperature, wind speed, and **precipitation**. Weather is always changing.

Climate is the pattern of weather over years or decades.

The climate in a desert is an arid, or very dry, climate.

Forecasting Weather Patterns

Scientists who study weather patterns are called **meteorologists**. They record weather data such as temperature and precipitation. They also track storms.

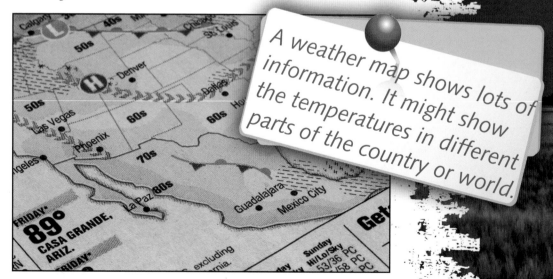

A weather map shows lots of information. It might show the temperatures in different parts of the country or world.

Some scientists actually chase storms. They want to learn how storms form and how fast they move.

7

Scientists who study climate are called **climatologists**. They study how the weather and climate were in the past to try and understand how they might be in the future.

Some climatologists study climate change and its future effects in the Arctic.

Meteorologists and climatologists use many tools to collect weather data.

Rain Gauge

A rain gauge measures the amount of rain that falls in one location.

Wind Sock

A wind sock attached to a pole shows which direction the wind is blowing.

Computers analyze the data collected by different tools to help meteorologists and climatologists forecast weather patterns and create climate models.

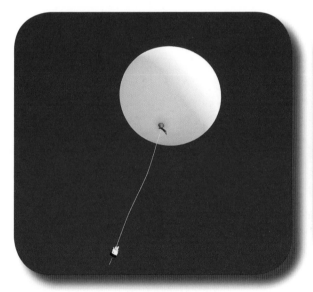

Weather Balloon

Scientists use weather balloons to carry special devices high into the sky to gather weather information.

Weather Satellite

Weather satellites orbit the Earth in outer space. They use cameras and other equipment to track all kinds of extreme weather.

Clouds give meteorologists clues about weather patterns. Clouds are made of water or ice droplets, too.

Stratus Clouds

Flat, gray clouds that hang low in the sky. Fog is a stratus cloud at ground level.

Cumulus Clouds

Big, white, fluffy clouds usually mean fair weather is ahead unless they grow tall, in which case it could become rainy.

When a cloud contains excess water or ice, it falls to Earth as precipitation. It can be rain, snow, sleet, or hail.

Cumulonimbus Clouds
These clouds often bring thunderstorms.

Cirrus Clouds
Thin, wispy clouds that form very high in the sky.

Extreme Weather

When too much or not enough precipitation falls, we can have extreme weather.

A **drought** occurs when there is lower than normal rainfall for an extended period of time.

When rain does not fall for months or years, the ground can dry out and crack apart.

15

A flood occurs when a lot of rain falls in a short time and water levels rise quickly. This can cause a stream, river, or lake to overflow its normal banks.

A flash flood has the fastest-moving water and can quickly demolish almost everything in its path.

Flood waters can destroy homes and cause lots of damage.

A **tornado** is a powerful rotating column of air that travels across the ground at speeds as high as 70 miles per hour (113 kilometers per hour). A tornado makes a roar as loud as a train.

A tornado's spinning funnel cloud is a powerful, destructive force.

Meteorologists use Doppler radar to help them predict the possible development of tornadoes and thunderstorms.

Hurricanes and typhoons are very powerful storms. When they hit land they can do great damage with their fierce winds, heavy rains, inland flooding, and huge waves crashing ashore.

Hurricane hunter airplanes fly right into the eye of a hurricane to study the massive storms.

This satellite image shows a hurricane covering most of the state of Florida.

FLORIDA

21

SHOW What You Know

1. What is the difference between weather and climate?

2. What kinds of tools do scientists use to study weather and climate?

3. Describe one kind of extreme weather.

Glossary

climate (KLYE-mit): weather typical of a place over a long period of time

climatologists (KLYE-muh-tahl-uh-jists): scientists who study weather patterns over long periods of time

drought (DROUT): a long period of time with reduced rainfall

hurricanes (HUR-I-kanez): violent storms with heavy rain and high winds

meteorologists (mee-tee-uh-RAH-luh-jists): scientists who study the Earth's atmosphere

precipitation (pri-sip-i-TAY-shuhn): water that falls from the sky in the form of rain, sleet, hail, or snow

tornado (tor-NAY-doh): a violent and very destructive windstorm that appears from a dark cloud shaped like a funnel

weather (WETH-ur): the condition of the atmosphere at a particular time and place

Index

Websites

www.theweatherchannelkids.com/
www.wxdude.com/kidres.html
www.tornadochaser.com
www.weatherwizkids.com"

Photo by Tom Story

About the Author

Conrad J. Storad is the award-winning author of more than 30 books for young readers. He writes about desert animals, plants, creepy crawlers, and planets. Conrad lives in Tempe, Arizona with his wife Laurie and their little double dapple wiener dog, Sophia. They love to explore Arizona's deserts and mountains.